The Real McCoy

The Life of an African-American Inventor

By Wendy Towle   *Paintings by* Wil Clay

SCHOLASTIC INC.
New York Toronto London Auckland Sydney

To Michael,
with love and thanks
— W.T.

To Melanie Darby for her
diligent and thorough
research for this book
— W.C.

The author wishes to acknowledge the Philadelphia Free Library Section for Government Documents; the curator and historian of the Ypsilanti Historical Society; and Betty Ann Wilson, the staff, and teachers at Nether Providence Elementary School for their help in researching this book.

The quotes in this book are from the Sept. 28, 1975, edition of the *Detroit Free Press*.

ISBN 0-590-48102-9

Text copyright © 1993 by Wendy Towle. Illustrations copyright © 1993 by Wil Clay. All rights reserved. Published by Scholastic Inc. BLUE RIBBON is a registered trademark of Scholastic Inc.

12 11 10 9 8 7 6 5 4 3 2   1   5 6 7 8 9/9

Printed in the U.S.A.   09

The illustrations in this books were painted on
canvas with acrylic paints.

Text design by Laurie Williams

Where did the expression "the real McCoy" come from? There are many legends surrounding the origin of this phrase, one of which revolves around Elijah McCoy, a successful African-American inventor. In his lifetime, Elijah McCoy patented over fifty inventions, none of which was more famous than his automatic oil cup, which eventually became standard equipment on most locomotives and heavy machinery. There were many imitations of McCoy's oil cup, but engineers knew that the model based on McCoy's design was the best of its kind. Hence, they asked for "the real McCoy." This may have been the inspiration for the expression which has come to mean the genuine article or "the real thing."

Many details about Elijah McCoy's personal life have been lost over the years. In some cases, biographical information has been scarce and often conflicting. The story of Elijah McCoy's life presented here reflects a composite of existing information we have been able to authenticate.

— W. T.

MICHIGAN

OHIO

INDIANA

UNDERGROUND RAILROAD

Elijah McCoy was born in Colchester, Ontario, Canada, on May 2, 1844, to George and Emillia McCoy, former slaves who had escaped from Kentucky via the Underground Railroad. The McCoys made the dangerous journey to Canada in search of freedom and a new home.

To support his growing family, Elijah's father, George McCoy, joined the Canadian Army and fought in the 1837 Rebel War. In return for his loyal service, he was given one hundred sixty acres of farmland. Elijah and his brothers and sisters were raised on this farm as free Canadian citizens.

KENTUCKY

DETROIT LAKE ST. CLAIR

CANADA

AMHERSTBURG

COLCHESTER

LAKE ERIE

ALL BLACK MILITIA

Educating their children was extremely important to Elijah's parents. The laws in the United States made it illegal for slaves to learn how to read and write. In their new country, the McCoys had high hopes for their children. They were property owners and, as a householder, George McCoy could vote, and could send his children to public school. Elijah attended a school for Black children in Colchester, Ontario, where he learned to read and write.

From a young age, Elijah was especially interested in the ways mechanical devices worked. He liked to take machines apart and put them back together.

Elijah's parents realized he had a special talent for working with tools and machines. They saved their money to send Elijah to a school where he could study mechanical engineering and could also learn how to design his own inventions. That school was in Edinburgh, Scotland. In 1860, when he was only sixteen years old, Elijah traveled three thousand miles across the Atlantic Ocean to study engineering in Scotland.

While Elijah was studying abroad, the Civil War in America broke out. President Lincoln issued the Emancipation Proclamation during the war. This was the first step toward freeing slaves in America. When the Civil War ended, Elijah could live anywhere in the United States as a free man. He finished his training in Scotland as a "master mechanic and engineer" and sailed to America.

Elijah settled in Ypsilanti, Michigan, but he had a hard time finding work as an engineer. Many people still thought of Blacks as slaves. They had never even heard of an educated Black person, not to mention a Black engineer. The only job Elijah could find was as a fireman/oilman for the Michigan Central Railroad.

In the late 1860s there were no cars, buses, or planes. People traveled by train. By our standards today, it was a slow and expensive way to travel. The trains were pulled by engines that ran on steam produced from water heated in huge boilers located in the cab of the locomotive. The fireman shoveled coal onto fires burning inside the firebox at the back of the cab. Every hour he shoveled over two tons of coal, scoop by scoop, into the firebox. He had to work quickly — if the fires burned out, the train would stop running. The fireman also had to monitor the level of the boiler water. If it was too low, pressure could build up and an explosion might occur. Elijah's job as a fireman was difficult and dangerous.

Elijah was also the oilman of the train. Parts of the train had to be oiled frequently so the train would run smoothly on the track. Every few miles, the train stopped. The oilman would walk the length of the train, oiling the axles, bearings, and other moving parts of each car. When the oilman finished lubricating the train parts, he raced back to the firebox in the cab to oversee the engine's needs.

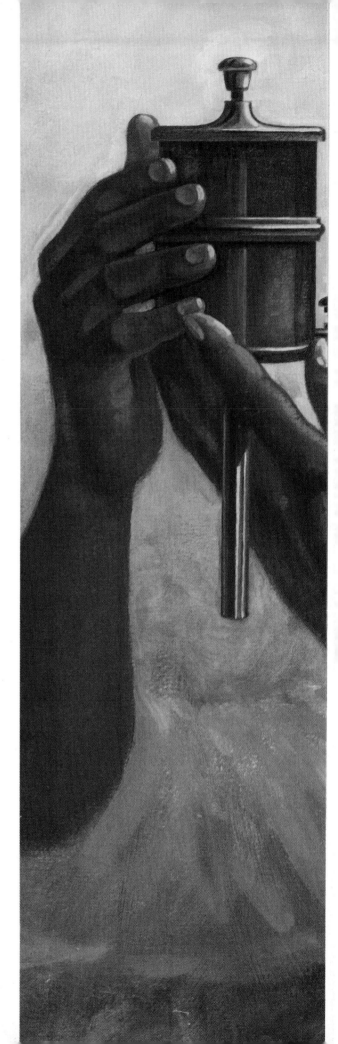

lijah wanted to make his job more efficient. Several men had already made devices that lubricated the train mechanically, but Elijah felt he could improve on those inventions. He worked for two years on his idea. Finally, he perfected a design of a lubricating cup that would automatically drip oil where it was needed. The train would no longer have to stop every few miles.

Elijah made his first oil cup model in 1872. He applied for a patent from the government to protect his rights to his invention.

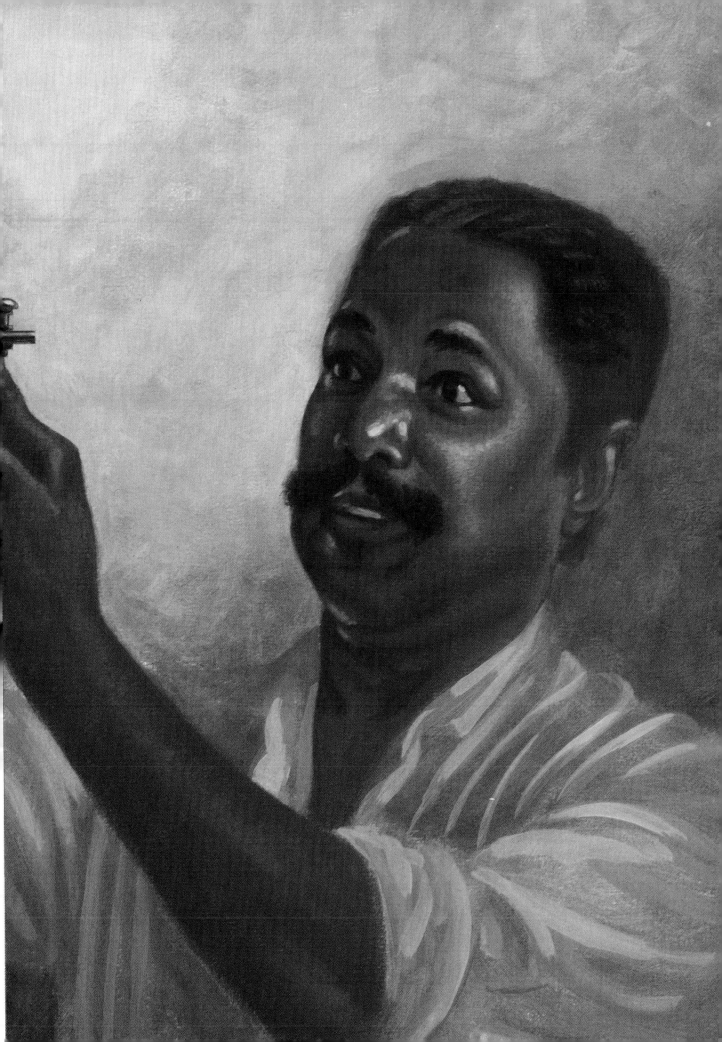

At first, many engineers were skeptical of Elijah's oil cup. They were not interested in the invention of a Black man. But the railroad owners at Michigan Central recognized that Elijah's design was superior to other models. Elijah's automatic oil cup was installed on their locomotives under his supervision. As the train engineers saw how well the McCoy cup worked, news of the successful invention spread. Soon, all the railroads wanted Elijah's automatic oil cup for their trains. Others tried to imitate Elijah McCoy's invention, but the engineers knew the difference. They always asked for "the real McCoy."

Elijah's oil cup made his job as oilman much easier. But Elijah wanted to spend more time working on his inventions. He wanted his own machine shop. To raise money, Elijah sold part of his patent on the oil cup to another investor. He only received a fraction of its worth, but the money enabled him to continue making mechanical devices. In the years to come, Elijah would sell other patents to finance his ideas for new inventions.

While he was working for the railroad and developing his oil cup, Elijah was also starting a family. Elijah married Ann Elizabeth Stewart in 1868. She died four years later, at the age of twenty-five. Elijah remarried in 1873, to Mary Eleanora Delaney. Like Elijah, she was the child of runaway slaves.

By 1882, Elijah was ready to leave the Michigan Central Railroad. He wanted to work full time on his inventions. The McCoys left Ypsilanti and settled in Detroit, Michigan, in an integrated neighborhood where the Mayor of Detroit, Barlum Thomas, also lived. Elijah served as a mechanical consultant to several firms, among them the Detroit Lubricating Company. He was highly respected. His expertise in his field was well known.

Elijah was dedicated to his work, but he also had time for young people, or "young whippersnappers" as he called them. He welcomed children to his office and showed them blueprints of his many inventions. John Roxburgh — who became manager to world-famous heavyweight boxer Joe Louis — remembers that Elijah always had advice for the young: "Stay in school. Be progressive. Work hard."

Elijah's wife Mary was also involved in community affairs. She was active in a number of charities, church clubs, and political organizations, as well as the women's suffrage movement, which sought the right for women to vote. Mary McCoy was the only Black charter member of the exclusive Twentieth Century Club, to which the most prominent women in Detroit belonged.

Although he continued to make improvements on his oil cup, Elijah also got ideas for new inventions from ordinary household tasks. When Mary needed a place to iron clothing, Elijah came up with the idea of an ironing table. This was probably the first portable ironing board.

When Elijah thought about finding a faster way to water the grass, he invented a lawn sprinkler. Even his own shoes gave him an idea. Elijah noticed that the rubber heels on his shoes wore out very quickly, so he decided to invent a better rubber heel. He also made designs for tires and tire treads. Elijah was so prolific that he sometimes patented two or three new devices in a year.

In 1916, Elijah developed the graphite lubricator, the invention of which he was most proud. At this time, a new type of locomotive — the superheater — was being used to pull trains. Elijah designed this new lubricator to oil the superheaters.

In 1920, Elijah McCoy established his own company — The Elijah McCoy Manufacturing Company — specifically to manufacture and sell his graphite lubricator. Shortly afterward, Elijah and Mary were involved in a traffic accident. Mary never fully recovered from her injuries and died in 1923.

Elijah grew lonely after Mary's death, and in the years that followed he used up what little money he had perfecting his inventions. His health worsened. In 1928, Elijah entered the Eloise Infirmary, a home for poor, elderly people. One year later, Elijah McCoy died. He was alone, and his famous achievements had been forgotten.

But Elijah McCoy's legacy to American technology and innovation remains with us today, in American homes and American industries. Variations of Elijah McCoy's oil cup are still used in factories, in mining and construction machinery, on naval boats, and even in space exploration vehicles.

In 1975, the city of Detroit celebrated Elijah McCoy Day by placing an historic marker at the site of his home and by naming a street — Elijah McCoy Drive — in his honor.

Lincoln

Elijah McCoy Dr

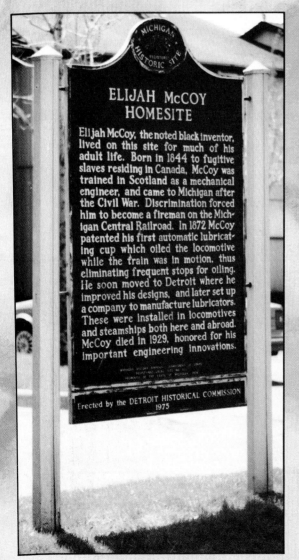

ELIJAH McCOY HOMESITE

Elijah McCoy, the noted black inventor, lived on this site for much of his adult life. Born in 1844 to fugitive slaves residing in Canada, McCoy was trained in Scotland as a mechanical engineer, and came to Michigan after the Civil War. Discrimination forced him to become a fireman on the Michigan Central Railroad. In 1872 McCoy patented his first automatic lubricating cup which oiled the locomotive while the train was in motion, thus eliminating frequent stops for oiling. He soon moved to Detroit where he improved his designs, and later set up a company to manufacture lubricators. These were installed in locomotives and steamships both here and abroad. McCoy died in 1929, honored for his important engineering innovations.

Erected by the DETROIT HISTORICAL COMMISSION
1975

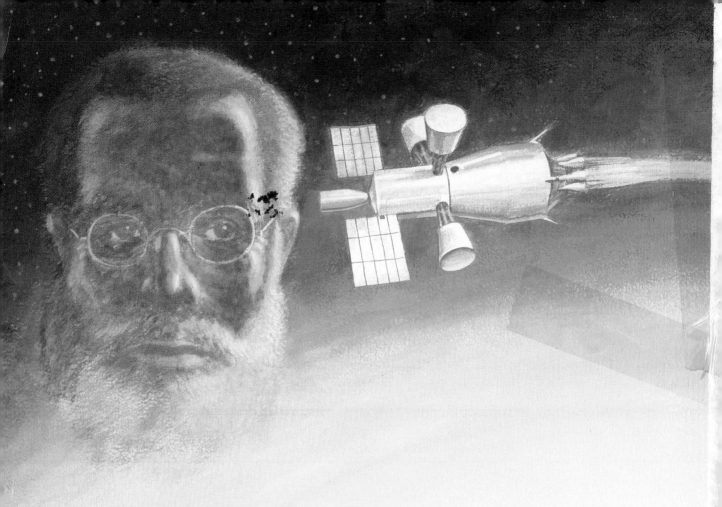

While he lived, Elijah McCoy was a role model for members of the Black community. A contemporary, Moses K. Fritz, recalled his admiration for this great man. "I looked on him with awe. I never knew a person of color who had done what he had done. He had accomplished something I never dreamed Negroes could do." As one of the first African-American inventors, Elijah McCoy's success story demonstrates one man's tremendous dedication to his work. It is fitting that his name — "the real McCoy" — has come to mean perfection.